An opi

LONDON
DELIS

Written by
SONYA BARBER

Photography by
DAVID POST

Monte's (no. 19)

INFORMATION IS DEAD.
LONG LIVE OPINION.

We tend to start these guides by asking: who cares about a guide book when everything you need to know can be found on the internet? And our answer is always: because in the mess of the internet you don't get expert information and concise opinion.

For this book you can replace 'guide book' with the word 'deli' and 'the internet' with 'the supermarket' and pose a similar question. And the answer to that new question is equally similar: because in the mess of the supermarket you don't get expert information and concise opinions.

You get our drift.

Other opinionated guides:

This page: Mestizo (no. 22)
Opposite: Good Things Deli (no. 16)

Lina Stores (no. 2)

Lulu's (no. 42)

BEST FOR...

A truly great sandwich
If you find yourself starving in the city centre, there's no better pitstop than I Camisa (no. 4) for freshly made Italian sandwiches. For the ultimate sarnie selection, nothing beats Paul Rothe & Son (no. 54) with hundreds of fillings on offer. Or, if you're craving authentic, made-on-site bagels stuffed with salt beef, make the journey to Shalom Hot Bagels (no. 28).

Drinks with friends
For small plates and a glass (or bottle) of something delicious, seek out Weino BIB (no. 12) where the wine is natural and low-impact. If you're in the mood for cocktails, order a marmalade martini at the lovely Lulu's (no. 42) or, on a sunny evening, bag a table outside Wilton Way Deli (no. 24) for a spritzy sundowner.

Gifts
Know someone who'd appreciate a stoneware jar of mustard or a beeswax-coated bread bag? Check out Peckham's own General Store (no. 41). Over at Honey & Spice (no. 49), there are colourful napkins and notebooks to be found as well as unbelievably moreish homemade biscuits. If you're feeling really generous, order a hamper of goodies from Panzer's (no. 10).

of a deli, they're often imagining a classic old-school Italian grocer with piles of pasta, panettones and parmesan. There are plenty of those included here, of course – but London's delis are much more diverse. Whether they're Colombian, Japanese or Jewish, all the delis in this book have a few things in common. They're specialists, selling hard-to-find produce and ingredients, and they all have a well-stocked counter or fridge with fresh finds and pre-prepared yummy things. Some are also cafes, supermarkets, wine bars, butchers, grocers or restaurants – but they all feel like they capture something of the essence of a deli.

Above all, delis are places filled with passion. Mostly independent, often run by dedicated generations of foodies, they're a true celebration of produce. Some are all about curating artisanal, sustainable, often local products, while others import ingredients and create dishes from across the world for London's many ex-pat communities.

In an age of supermarket homogeneity, delis can provide cooking inspiration with new flavours as well as a taste of home. And without meaning to get all David Attenborough about it, the sad truth is that many are struggling – with the Covid hangover, Brexit headaches and painful rent increases, even the most beloved delis are having trouble and need support. So, if you want an excuse to go splurge your latest paycheck on some delicious food that will make you very, *very* happy, please pay a visit to one of these fine establishments – and say hi from us.

Sonya Barber, 2023

EAT YOUR WAY THROUGH LONDON'S DELIS

I've been going to London's delis since I was a kid. On weekends, my parents would schlep across the city for homemade Italian pumpkin ravioli, fresh bagels or that brand of salty French butter that you could only get at this one place. As a child, these trips were an exciting adventure filled with colourful packets of fun-looking things stacked way above my head, salamis swinging from the ceiling, shiny counters to press my sticky hands against and always a tasty snack at the end.

Today, I still get a similar thrill visiting a new deli, peering hungrily into fridges packed with goodies, snaffling ingredients I've never heard of (let alone cooked with), treating myself to a block of posh truffle-laced cheese and salivating as containers are stuffed with fresh dips, olives and sweet treats. If I could afford it, that's where I would do all my shopping. Forget Michelin-starred restaurants, I think some of London's best food can be found in your local deli.

There are delis in most London neighbourhoods and all play a different role – some platform local, independent producers and others have been cornerstones in the community for decades. And people are rightly passionate about their favourites, travelling all the way to the end of the tube line for a certain ingredient, bragging about their finds on Instagram and showing off cute branded tote bags. And yes, I do all these things too.

Most dictionary definitions of 'delicatessen' mention cold meats and cheeses and fine foreign produce. When people think

A picnic

Pick up fluffy pita and herby dips at Oren (no. 31) for a long lunch in London Fields or just grab a veggie sausage roll and an ice cream sandwich at The Deli Downstairs (no. 27) and take a stroll in Victoria Park. Got a date? Find antipasti and a bottle of fizz at Monte's (no. 19) for a romantic picnic in Highbury Fields.

Sweet treats

In need of a sugar hit? Well, you will be spoilt for choice. Eat your way through every flavour of Portuguese custard tart at Madeira (no. 33), scoff down sticky Greek cakes at Athenian Grocery (no. 50) or stock up on stacks of baklava at Phoenicia (no. 6). And let's not forget Luigi's (no. 55) famous tiramisu…

A spot of lunch

For a steaming bowl of ravioli, nab a table at London's original Italian deli Terroni (no. 1) or low-key south London hero Di Lieto (no. 44). If you're in the mood for cosy comfort food, there's no place better than the Quality Chop House Cafe & Shop (no. 3) for French onion soup and a superior club sandwich.

Ambitious cooks

Try your hand at sushi after a trip to Japan Centre (no. 46) for bamboo rolling mats and speciality fish. All the Persian spices required to make your own ghormeh sabzi can be sourced at beloved indie Persepolis (no. 36). And there's no excuse not to nail the perfect pasta thanks to Salvino (no. 20), just ask the friendly staff for tips.

1

TERRONI OF CLERKENWELL

A taste of the old country

Back in Victorian times, Clerkenwell was London's first Little Italy and Terroni, founded there in 1878, proudly calls itself the capital's original Italian deli. Two doors down from the ornate St Peter's Italian Church, these days it's part-deli, part-cafe: at lunchtime, the tables are full of regulars tucking into bruschette, bresaola salad and steaming ravioli. Here, you'll find ingredients from across *il bel paese*. There's a counter for olives, another for cheeses and meats, and a third for food to go – sample the fried arancini, then try one their ricotta-filled sfogliatelle. Let's hope Terroni sticks around for at least another century.

138 Clerkenwell Road, EC1R 5DL
Nearest station: Farringdon
terroni.co.uk

2
LINA STORES

Prestige Italian deli chain

Back in the day, Lina Stores was an old-school deli with a ceiling covered in low-hanging hams. Then in 2018, it had a serious glow-up: the iconic façade of turquoise tiles became part of a slick rebrand that launched an in-house range of produce and a handful of pasta restaurants. Does it feel a bit more corporate? Yes. Is the food any good? Absolutely. Come here to sample regional cheeses and hams, beautifully crimped fresh ravioli and homemade sauces. It's also a great place to find gifts, like colourful tins of amaretti or bottled negroni – though there are still enough dangling meats to give you a mild concussion.

18 Brewer Street, W1F 0SG
Nearest station: Tottenham Court Road
Other locations: Multiple, see website
linastores.co.uk

3

THE QUALITY CHOP HOUSE CAFE & SHOP

A British institution reimagined

There's been a chop house on this spot serving traditional grub to hungry Londoners since 1869. These days, the iconic Grade II-listed benches remain but the menu is far more contemporary, while still celebrating British classics of course. The lovingly curated shop and butcher next door are an extension of their passion for comfort food so there are plenty of QCH dishes to take home: steak and ale pies, their legendary confit potatoes, pastrami salmon, pork pies and rice pudding – with handwritten labels. There are also modern pantry staples, fresh veg and a big butcher's block at the back ready to slice up whatever cut you're after.

88-90 Farringdon Road, EC1R 3EA
Nearest station: Farringdon
cafe.thequalitychophouse.com

4

I CAMISA & SON

The best spaghetti in Soho

When the owners announced they were closing this 100-year-old deli due to rent increases, there were audible sobs from across the city. But after negotiating with their landlord, the self-proclaimed 'first real Italian food store' lives on to serve homesick Italians (and those in-the-know) classic produce from Sicily to Piedmont. It's not particularly big or glamorous but it's got all the good stuff: homemade tortellini, pesto and bolognese, creamy burrata and festive panettone swinging from the ceiling. Don't miss out on their sandwiches, made fresh with any meat and cheese of your choosing, wrapped in blue-and-white chequered paper and only costing a fiver.

61 Old Compton Street, W1D 6HS
Nearest station: Leicester Square
icamisa.co.uk

5

FURANXO

A slick Spanish edit

Giving the traditional Andalucian *ultramarinos* (grocer) a trendy makeover, Furanxo has two London locations showcasing their refined selection of produce from independent farmers, popular snacks in beautifully designed packets and stellar haul of natural wines – all sourced from Spain. Pick up colourful (and TikTok-friendly) tins of razor clams or sardines, cloth bags of dried beans and bottles of salty, health-giving Vichy Catalan sparkling water made even more delicious with a glug of vermouth. Find wine-washed goat's cheese and hand-sliced chorizo, morcilla and Ibérico ham, before pausing to grab a bottle of organic Rioja – everything you need for a date night.

63 Exmouth Market, EC1R 4QL
Nearest station: Angel
Other location: Dalston
furanxo.com

coppa Ibérica Bellota
£7.90

Lomo Ibérico
£6.90

6

PHOENICIA

A slice of the Med in NW5

You can find just about anything in this friendly food hall which has an emphasis on Greek and Lebanese cuisine but sells everything from brightly coloured macarons to laksa paste. The store is split into an exceptionally diverse supermarket and a fresh deli counter – but there's also a halal butcher, a cabinet of spinning rotisserie chickens, a refill station with a cheeky nougat shelf and a stellar selection of olives from Greece, Lebanon, Spain and Morocco. This is the place to stock up on great mezze so head to the counter for tubs of dolmades, grilled aubergine salad, herby tabouleh, kibbeh and as much sticky baklava as you can carry.

186-192 Kentish Town Road, NW5 2AE
Nearest station: Kentish Town
phoeniciafoodhall.co.uk

7

DA MARIO

A pasta lover's dream

Filled, dried, gluten-free and layered in a lasagne – there's a lot of pasta going on at this north London stalwart. The shelves are piled with shapes way beyond the usual twists and tubes while the counter gleams with inviting-looking fresh tortellini stuffed with decadent fillings like pecorino and honey or wild boar. This small-but-mighty store is packed full of toothsome eats: tiramisu and arancini, olives and antipasti, cheeses and rustic grissini, and Oddono's unmissable gelati. They only accept minimum card payments of £10, but you won't have any trouble spending that – and more.

34 Highbury Park, N5 2AA
Nearest station: Arsenal

8
NATURAL NATURAL

All the goods for a sushi feast

You can pick up ramen noodles and a packet of frozen gyoza almost anywhere, but if you want to delve a bit deeper into Japanese cooking then head to Natural Natural. It not only stocks rare and imported packaged goods, but also all the fresh ingredients you could ever need – from slabs of raw tuna to salad-revolutionising daikon. And if you feel like cooking, there's a huge array of food-to-go, from onigiri stuffed with pickled plum to bento boxes and chicken skewers as well as an impressive range of sake (and that's just a fragment of the booze on offer at their specialist sake and sashimi store in Ealing Common). Going on a weekend? Bring something to read, the queue can get long – but it will be worth it.

1 Goldhurst Terrace, NW6 3HX
Nearest station: Finchley Road
Other location: Ealing
natural-natural.shop

20

SAKE
BEER
SHOCHU
PLUM WINE
FRUIT LIQUEUR
WHISKEY
GIN

9

HOFFMAN'S

Traditional Jewish fishmonger

If you know your Jewish delis, you're probably familiar with the red-and-white tubs of Hoffman's fishy deli delights. What you might not know is that this unassuming Stamford Hill store is where the magic happens. It's predominantly a fishmonger with whole cod, haddock and plaice on ice, ready to be filleted by the expert staff. There are also breaded fillets, big bowls of minced salmon, gefilte fish and a freezer full of frozen parcels, but head to the fridge for chopped herring, potato salad, sweet fish balls, jars of tartar sauce and extra strong beetroot and horseradish chrayne: the perfect accompaniment to fresh fish.

92 Oldhill St, N16 6NA
Nearest station: Stamford Hill

10

PANZER'S

Deluxe deli with NYC-style nosh

Panzer's is the closest thing in London to a gourmet New York Jewish deli. The 75-year-old institution sells perfectly chewy 'everything' bagels, mouthwatering salt beef sandwiches and nourishing chicken soup with matzo balls. Check out the counter for tubs of scallion schmear, dressed salads, crispy chicken schnitzel or even some chopped liver to slather on toasted rye bread. Catering to the diverse but upmarket tastes of St John's Wood, Panzer's is also a seriously well-stocked food hall: find continental cheeses, an aisle of American junk food and even a sushi bar.

13-19 Circus Road, NW8 6PB
Nearest station: St John's Wood
panzers.co.uk

SOUP & SALAD   CHARCUTERIE

GRANADILLO
£2.50

Red Cherry
Plums
£6.95/KILO

VIGNOLA

SUSINA PLUM PRUNE PFLAUME CIRUELA

VIGNOLA

11

MELROSE
AND MORGAN

Posh treats aplenty

This mini-chain of north London delis has a serious USP: an extensive house range of groceries made in small batches from mostly British ingredients. Aesthetically pleasing red-and-white jars of ketchup, pickles and jams are neatly arranged alongside packets of their moreish granola, crackers, chocolates and biscuits. But they don't just sell their own snacks, other London-based producers get a look in too, including Secret Smokehouse, Hackney Gelato and La Fromagerie. There are quiches, salads, sandwiches and cakes to eat in or take away. But buyers beware, the quality of the products is high – with the price tags to match.

42 Gloucester Avenue, NW1 8JD
Nearest station: Chalk Farm
Other location: Hampstead
melroseandmorgan.com

Try our Picnic
for Two filled
with British
Classics and
everything you
need for the
perfect afternoon
in the park
£44.95

12
WEINO BIB

Dine-in deli serving low-waste natural wine

Sustainable booze is at the heart of this all-in-one taproom, deli and restaurant, whether it's craft ales from round the corner or bag-in-a-box natural wine. But this is so much more than just a posh off-licence. Weino BIB stocks everything you'd expect from a Dalston deli: carefully curated cheeses, salami and ginormous tins of Perelló olives. During the day you can sit in for a plate of whatever takes your fancy from a counter chock-full of homemade pies and savoury sausage rolls. By night, the lights dim and the open kitchen starts turning out small plates and big platters all served with a glass of something (genuinely) good.

39 Balls Pond Road, N1 4BW
Nearest station: Dalston Junction
weinobib.co.uk

13

DE BEAUVOIR DELI

Gourmet deli championing small producers

Straddling Islington and Hackney, De Beauvoir is a chic neighbourhood with just a bit of edge, and its (somewhat bougie) centre of gravity is this much-loved deli. Behind its signature blue frontage you'll find a tick list of favourites: Dusty Knuckle's deliciously flaky cinnamon sugar-coated morning buns, La Tua Pasta, Suffolk-based Pump Street chocolate, Neal's Yard cheeses and organic fruit and veg. But it's the lunchtime sandwiches that draw the biggest queues at the hatch, although they are always worth the wait. Try the Veggie New Yorker, such a local legend that it's inspired its own t-shirt.

98 Southgate Road, N1 3JD
Nearest station: Haggerston
thedebeauvoirdeli.co.uk

14

SUPERETTE

A who's who of London food

It might look like a retro laundrette, but this Highbury hotspot is actually a fun mega mix of goodies from some of the capital's best suppliers: there's potato sourdough from Dusty Knuckle, St. John's custard-filled doughnuts, coffee from Climpson's, glass bottles of milk from the Estate Dairy and fresh seafood from Bourne's – plus plenty of other snacks, pickles, nibbles, condiments, chocolates and pre-prepped food from independent makers. There's also a tour-de-force of infinitely quaffable natural wine – including sparkling from London's own Renegade winery – and hearty toasties (made with melty cheese from La Fromagerie, of course).

165 Upper Street, N1 1US
Nearest station: Highbury & Islington
Other location: Highgate
superettestore.com

15

LE COQ EPICIER

French expat fave

When a regular comes in and orders 'une baguette', you know you're in the right place for authentic French food. This unassuming deli on Camden Passage leans heavily into the classics, with enough foie gras, confit duck, rich terrine and fish pâté to satisfy the most extravagant gastronome. In the fridge, look out for blocks of crunchy salted butter, crème caramels and bottles of sparkling fizz. Yes, it's all artery clogging decadence – but that's what makes it one of the world's best cuisines.

1 Camden Passage, N1 8EA
Nearest station: Angel
lecoqepicier.co.uk

16

GOOD THINGS DELI

Bagels, babka and fun Jewish bites

The queues for bagels at The Good Egg restaurant got so ridiculous they had to open a spin-off up the road specialising in the boiled beauties. This deli lives up to its honorific with a concise, punchy menu of hot and cold filled bagels. Try the not-at-all-kosher harissa, bacon and egg mayo or the matzo-coated fried fish (aka a posh fishfinger sandwich), and there are moreish deli pots too, such as roasted garlic hummus and pistachio butter. You'll find fancy Middle Eastern ingredients like black tahini and sour cherry molasses, but the main attraction here is the unbeatably gooey chocolate-rippled babka – snap it up before they run out.

56 Stoke Newington Church Street, N16 0NB
Nearest station: Stoke Newington
thegoodegg.co/good-things-deli

17

KOLLOS

One-stop-sklep for Eastern European staples

Partial to a smoked sausage? Fancy frying up some potato-and-cheese-filled pierogi? Well, this popular Polish grocer has one of the best selections we've ever seen. There's enough pork belly, lardo and pâté in the extensive deli here to satisfy the hungriest shopper – but Kollos is not just for carnivores, there's also a plentiful array of pickles and kraut sold by weight and smoked cheeses as well as traditional gingerbread, satisfyingly sweet jams and a vast range of vodka to keep in the freezer for a rainy day. The staff know their stuff, so don't be afraid to ask questions.

Abney Park Terrace,
Stoke Newington High Street, N16 7HU
Nearest station: Stoke Newington
kollos.business.site

Ogórek
4,99
zł

18

NOURISHED COMMUNITIES

Veg shop-turned-community minded deli

If you want a feel-good shopping experience, it doesn't get more wholesome than this unpretentious deli. What started out as a lockdown veg box scheme has now bloomed into a wonderful local store showcasing seasonal produce from the UK's finest independent producers and farmers. There are enough basics here to do your weekly shop, but it's the treats that will keep you coming back: ice cream sandwiches from Happy Endings, fennel and garlic salami cured in London and creamy, hand-rolled butter. Plus, they still do a reasonably priced fruit and veg box, as well as yoga classes and climate crisis workshops in their King's Cross cafe. Right on.

263 Upper Street, N1 2UQ
Nearest station: Highbury & Islington
Other locations: Arsenal, King's Cross, Walthamstow
nourishedcommunities.com

19

MONTE'S

High-end Italian specialist

With its pristine glass counter, displays of Dolce & Gabbana-branded Sicilian sweets and high ceiling (and, *ahem*, prices), Monte's could be mistaken for a luxury boutique. But it's not all about the aesthetic – and there's nothing superficial about their friendly welcome or passion for Italian fare. They stock regional specialities and artisanal produce, always of the highest quality, whether it's jars of demi-glacé cherries or fig and walnut biscotti. Raid the aforementioned glass counter for truffled pecorino and homemade rocket pesto – and look out for the framed photo of the owners with the ultimate gourmand: Danny DeVito.

23 Canonbury Lane, N1 2AS
Nearest station: Highbury & Islington
montesdeli.com

Banderillas

Marinade anchovies wrapped around green olives stuffed with red peppers.

£23.00 kg (£2.30 100g)

20

SALVINO

Just like mamma used to make

Opened in 1979 by the Sicilian Salvino brothers, this north London family-run deli is a deeply authentic Italian experience. There's pasta as far as the eye can see, big bags of dark-roasted coffee beans, a survey of Italian wine from Barolo to Vermentino, and a flourishing collection of Italian seeds so you can grow your own basil and rocket at home. The staff are passionate about their pesto and will make you a memorable sandwich which you can enjoy on the little tables outside, followed by an espresso so strong that you'll be bouncing along the street after.

47 Brecknock Road, N7 0BT
Nearest station: Kentish Town
salvino.co.uk

Mostarda

SALVO

Nocellara
9.99
1kg

Capers
Salted
1.25

Sicilian
Pine Nuts
2.49

Siciliano
2.25

Calabria
2.25

Ascola
2.25

DANGER

Salsicciamo

5.99

Baci

Baci

Baci

"A gorgeously detailed romance!"
Disarmingly beautiful!
IL POSTINO
SALAMI
NEGRONI
PARMIGIANO REGGIANO
PARMIGIANO REGGIANO
2.79
GORGONZOLA
MOZZARELLA
1.25
6.99
ACQUA PANNA

21

GALLO NERO

A slice of rustic Italy

There's a good chance that you'll spot a real life *nonna* in this family-run favourite chatting animatedly to the owner Michael. Keeping Stoke Newingtonites in parmesan and olives since 1988, Gallo Nero brings together hard-to-find delicacies like cuttlefish ink and rum baba with classic Italian meats and cheeses. The wooden shelves are laden with Sicilian olive oil (sold on tap) and row upon row of dried pasta, including the longest spaghetti you'll ever see, as well as all the aperitivi ingredients you need for a long summer evening.

45 Newington Green Road, N1 4QT
Nearest station: Canonbury
Other location: Stoke Newington
*@galloneroitaliandeli_*

22

MESTIZO MEXICAN MARKET

Friendly Mexican mini-mart

Surprisingly, there's a slice of sunny Mexico just off Euston Road. Whether you want to make tacos or fajitas – or just get a seriously good bottle of tequila blanco – this colourful store has everything you need for a fiesta: salsas and hot sauces, frijoles, humongous bags of tortilla chips and over ten different varieties of dried chilli. There's also a cast of big Day of the Dead skeletons, cacti and a massive fake Chihuahua to keep you company as you browse. Feeling lazy? Check the freezer for stuffed tamales and Mexican ready meals. Or, if you're too hungry to wait, head to their vibrant restaurant next door.

101 Hampstead Road, NW1 3EL
Nearest station: Warren Street
mestizomarket.com

Aqui
Puro Producto
Perrón

Hay que empezar
el día con Huevos
frijolitos, chiles
y ... con
cerveza
no hay...

23

L'EAU À LA BOUCHE

Francophile foodie favourite

If the smoked garlic and hanging strings of onions don't give it away, La Bouche is a deeply French store (with a smattering of choice Spanish and Italian goodies thrown in). The fromage counter is manned by a deli maestro who prompts indecisive punters for their orders of oozy bries and delicate gruyère. But don't be rushed. There are plenty of gastronomic classics packed into this busy shop and café worth lingering over: mini madeleines, saucisson, bottles of Calvados, Breton fish soup and jars of gloriously fatty pâté. Order a croque monsieur and grab a table outside for Parisian-style people-watching on Broadway Market.

35-37 Broadway Market, E8 4PH
Nearest station: London Fields
labouche.co.uk

CORNICHONS
£1.50/100g

FRENCH SAUCISSON

DIANA's
LONDON
SEA SALT
CARAMEL
EASTER

HERITAGE
MIXED
TOMATOES
£9.95/Kg

24

WILTON WAY DELI

Hackney community linchpin

Wilton Way is one of the most villagey streets in Hackney and this deli is very much at the heart of it. There's a cafe with bustling alfresco tables serving matcha lattes and melted taleggio sandwiches to cheery locals, and a small shop just a few doors down with a heavily edited selection of European treats and east London favourites like Willy's Pies, made round the corner in London Fields. At night, the shop transforms into an intimate restaurant hosting pasta parties, burger nights, pottery sessions and literary salons, but it's also just a lovely spot for a sundowner negroni or two.

63 and 67 Wilton Way, E8 1BG
Nearest station: Hackney Central
wiltonwaydeli.com

25

4 COSE

Artist-curated storecupboard essentials

After starting out by 'dealing' delicious parmigiano reggiano in 2015, artists Charlotte Cullinan and Jeanine Richards and art director Andrea Sassi opened their small art-filled grocery store on the gallery-heavy Vyner Street in 2017. The concept is simple: focus on the *quatre cose* (four things) key to making a great meal – exceptional parmesan, pasta, olive oil and salami – and sell only one type of each. The lack of choice is wonderfully refreshing, although they do stock a few other bits and bobs like 'nduja paste, coppa ham, arborio rice and panettone – if you have any change after investing in a £30 chunk of the 'king of cheese'.

7 Vyner Street, E2 9DG
Nearest station: Cambridge Heath
4cose.london

26

PROVISIONS

Lesser-spotted cheese and wine

Provisions is a serious French deli. They're serious about what they sell, and the products are seriously good. Gazing into the vast expanse of the cheese fridge might send you into a fromage frenzy but the staff are on hand to help, whether you're after an unpasteurised buttery blue or a nutty goat. Hugo, the charismatic owner, sources as much as possible from artisan producers *and* they import most of the biodynamic wines themselves, so there's stuff here you won't get anywhere else. Take your time and discover plenty more treats, like greengage jam and chestnut purée (for the most feast-worthy toast), to indulge yourself with.

308 Hackney Road, E2 7SJ
Nearest station: Hoxton
Other location: Holloway
provisionslondon.co.uk

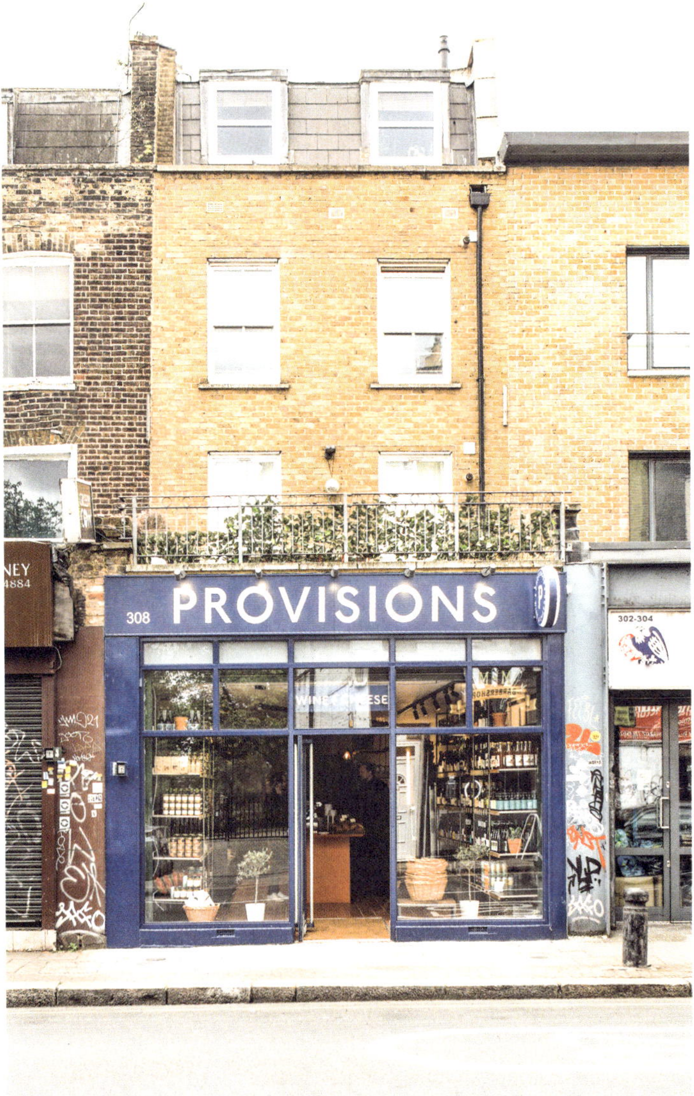
308
PROVISIONS
302-304

HARD PA...

SHEEP

BLOOMY RIND

LIVAROT AO...
AU LAIT CR...

FROMAGERIE BLANC

ÉPOISSES

Gauger

ÉPOISSES

Gauger

27

THE DELI DOWNSTAIRS

Sustainably minded village shop

Community and climate change are high on the agenda at this corner spot in Victoria Park Village. Don't be fooled by the old-fashioned hand-painted sign, this deli is bang up-to-date with its 100 per cent renewable energy, plant-based compostable packaging, refill stations and ban on disposable coffee cups. Worthiness aside, there are many delectable reasons to visit, from pre-prepped dishes like lasagne and sustainable fishcakes to cheese, charcuterie and locally sourced goodies. Look out for London Fermentary's crunchy krauts and Thai curry pastes from Farang in Highbury. Once you've finished browsing, grab a top-notch savoury pastry for a walk in Victoria Park.

211 Victoria Park Road, E9 7JN
Nearest station: London Fields
thedelidownstairs.co.uk

28

SHALOM HOT BAGELS

Ashkenazi classics in the east London suburbs

Chances are you won't be randomly passing by this one, but it's well worth a special excursion. This classic British Jewish deli has been boiling bagels since 1986 and still sells everything you need for a kosher-style spread: platzels covered in caramelised onions, tubs of crunchy new green pickles, sweet fried fish balls, chopped herring, slabs of smoked salmon, New York-style cheesecake, potato latkes and freshly filled salt beef bagels (or beigels, as many of the regulars still call them). There's always a queue and the staff don't like dawdlers so have a good idea of what you want before you reach the front.

35 Woodford Avenue, Ilford, IG2 6UF
Nearest station: Gants Hill
shalomhotbeigels.com

29
PINCH LA DELI

Spaghetti and udon united at last

Japanese and Italian cuisines may not be obvious bedfellows but they're perfectly paired at this Leyton newcomer opened by Italian restaurant manager Eihab and his wife Hiromi. Wasabi crisps sit happily next to olive oil breadsticks, while gnocchi and miso fight for space in the fridge – but there's also a strong French contingent here with hefty wedges of Morbier, saucisson and stylish Mariage Frères teas all making an appearance. Look out for fresh pasta and other Italian classics prepared daily alongside a small selection of Asian dishes (including a perfectly spicy kimchi) to eat in or take away.

312 Lea Bridge Road, E10 7LD
Nearest station: Lea Bridge
pinchladeli.com

30

GERMAN DELI

Wieners in a warehouse

You could easily miss the modest sign alerting you to this European enclave hidden in an industrial estate selling Deutsch condiments and larder staples to loyal customers. There are freshly baked pretzels and cakes, including creamy and surprisingly not sickly-sweet German bienenstich cake and poppyseed crumble. Oh, and then there's their impressive selection of cooking, slicing and spreading sausages, including smoked salami, veal liver pâté and gooey cheese-stuffed wurst. Be sure to stock up on curry ketchup too so you can satisfy that currywurst craving without booking a trip to Berlin.

Unit 11, Forest Trading Estate, Priestley Way, E17 6AL
Nearest station: Blackhorse Road
germandeli.co.uk

31

OREN DELICATESSEN

Tel Aviv-inspired restaurant offshoot

Three years after opening his acclaimed Dalston restaurant, Israeli chef Oded Oren has followed up with a deli, inviting you to bring his refined Tel Avivian flavours home. In a stark concrete-floored space stand two fridges stuffed with mouthwatering house-made meze in takeaway tubs that are great for quick lunches or lazy suppers, while the opposite wall is dedicated to an impressive collection of natural wine. A kitchen at the back dishes up fresh pita and challah bread, plus tempting takeaways including hummus with spiced mutton mince and buns stuffed with chopped liver or schmaltz herring. It's easy to spend money here, but worth it to convince friends that you've suddenly become the next Ottolenghi.

6c Ada Street, E8 4QU
Nearest station: London Fields
orendeli.com

32

YARDARM

The pride of Leyton

Yardarm is still one of the most beloved spots on Leyton's buzzy Francis Road – despite having a lot of competition from other trendy newcomers in recent years. During the day you can pop in for a strong coffee and a quiche (you'll find the seats at the back, as well as a tiny garden shaded by grapevines) or peruse posh La Tua pasta, John's of Dalston pizza and Epping Forest Honey harvested just up the road. If you're after something stronger, Yardarm also moonlights as a wine bar serving glasses of chilled orange wine and frothy Cava alongside plates of grilled sardines and pork pies with English mustard – all until a very respectable 8.30pm. Bliss.

238 Francis Road, E10 6NQ
Nearest station: Leyton
yardarm.london

33

MADEIRA

Portuguese treasure trove

Occupying not one but *three* cavernous railway arches, this restaurant, cafe and comprehensively stocked deli and bakery is its very own *little* Little Portugal. All the different regions are represented – the booze selection alone has Madeiran punch, port from Porto and cherry liqueur from Lisbon. Browse the aisles to find everything from classic tinned fish, salt cod and feijoada (a hearty traditional bean stew) to freshly baked marble cakes and trays of gooey custard tarts in blueberry, raspberry, matcha and passionfruit flavours. It's only right to try one of each.

46c Albert Embankment, SE1 7TL
Nearest station: Vauxhall
madeiralondon.co.uk

34

DELICATESSEN SERRANA

Community hub in Little Portugal

It might reside on the deafening A3, but step inside Serrana and you'll feel like you're back on holiday in a Lisbon mini-mart. The salt cod fridge takes pride of place – as it should – next to a counter crammed with salami (both the meat and chocolate varieties), sugary cakes and traditional Iberian lunch fodder like chicken escalope and breaded swordfish. Other rooms lie beyond, replete with wine and covetable terracotta tableware. Most customers will be speaking Portuguese, and everyone seems to know each other – so stick around for a bica coffee and make some friends.

224 Clapham Road, SW9 0PZ
Nearest station: Stockwell
@delicatessenserrana

35

CHATICA

Latin American cafe and provisions

Just off the Elephant and Castle roundabout, a series of railway arches hosts a thriving hub of bars, shops and restaurants serving south London's multinational Latin American community. Chatica's arch is mostly taken up by a friendly cafe where baskets of deep-fried empanadas and sweet pastries whizz out from the kitchen. At the back, a storeroom-like shop stocks all the essentials: tortillas, corn tamale wrappers, salsas and a house-brand range that's great for anyone who's not sure where to start. In the unlikely event that you can't find what you're looking for, head to DistriAndina a few doors down for an even bigger selection with more of a supermarket vibe.

2 Elephant Road, SE17 1LB
Nearest station: Elephant & Castle
chatica.co

36

PERSEPOLIS

Idiosyncratic Middle Eastern cafe and larder

With its unmissable yellow shop front, this Peckham emporium is a labour of love by eccentric chef and cookbook author Sally Butcher and her husband Jamshid. Much of the space is a laid-back vegetarian cafe with a living room vibe serving mezze and stews at pleasingly reasonable prices. But its heart is the 'corner shop': a cornucopia of Iranian and Middle Eastern ingredients, treats and paraphernalia, where shisha pipes sit atop a rack of sabzi herbs. Whatever you buy, whether it's saffron ice cream, a backgammon board, a bag of dried limes or a ceramic tagine pot, try at least one of the Persian shirini (sweets).

28-30 Peckham High Street, SE15 5DT
Nearest station: Peckham Rye
foratasteofpersia.co.uk

37

BOROUGH MARKET

The mother of all delis

London's biggest deli isn't really a deli at all: it's Southwark's thousand-year-old food market where farmers have been selling their wares since at least 1014. These days, however, the focus is on artisanal delicacies from around the world. Grab your sturdiest tote bag and travel from the Dordogne (truffles) to Calabria ('nduja) and the Baltic (rye bread). There are stalls specialising in everything from spices to game meat, plus the market's traditional strength: British fruit and veg. It really is the capital's greatest food destination so give it a full day, fuelling up on Monmouth coffee and a square of halva at The Turkish Deli as needed.

8 Southwark Street, SE1 1TL
Nearest station: London Bridge
boroughmarket.org.uk

38

ITALO

Legendary anarchic deli-cafe

Just off the hellish Vauxhall Gyratory is Bonnington Square, a peaceful enclave of Victorian terraces squatted in the 1970s which continues today as a cooperative. The countercultural spirit is alive and well at Italo, where well-worn wooden shelves are stacked with affordable Italian goodies and draped with anti-Boris bunting. At weekends, a diverse crowd packs in for coffee and delicious breakfast sandwiches – grab an alfresco table by the square's volunteer-run garden and browse the tiny Italo newsletter that gives all the latest from the shop and the community. Now that really is the good life.

13 Bonnington Square, SW8 1TE
Nearest station: Vauxhall
italodeli.co.uk

39

BRINDISA

The most famous Spanish deli in London

You'll have seen Brindisa's own-brand products all over deli and supermarket aisles – they have been importing the best of Spain since 1988, after all. But for the full experience, head to their flagship deli in Borough Market. The high-ceilinged warehouse is packed almost to the rafters with all the Iberian big hitters: a cabinet of Perelló olives here, an extensive selection of Torres crisps there, a cheese counter going *way* beyond Manchego and a full-on Ibérico ham carvery. For sweet-toothed types there's also plentiful nougat and figgy treats, but it's the hot chorizo rolls, served every lunchtime from Thursday to Saturday, that are the real showstoppers.

Floral Hall, Borough Market, Stoney Street, SE1 9AF
Nearest station: London Bridge
Other location: Balham
brindisa.com

40
GLADWELL'S

Relaxed neighbourhood grocerant

If you're going to open a deli, taking over a former bank is a pretty great idea. The ceilings are high, there are lovely arch windows, and, best of all, the old vault in the basement makes an ideal wine cellar for hosting private 'lock in' tasting sessions. It's no wonder that grocer-restaurant Gladwell's has quickly become a local favourite. Find fromage from Borough Market's Mons Cheesemongers and smoked salmon from 100-year-old east London institution H. Forman & Son. There's also a chilled cafe at the front so once you've finished shopping, settle in for a kimchi and cheese toastie with the bottle of wine you've just bought – corkage-free.

2 Camberwell Church Street, SE5 8QU
Nearest station: Denmark Hill
gladwells.co.uk

41

GENERAL STORE

Peckham's trendy village shop

You'll find this elegant grocery on Bellenden
Road, a low-key residential row parallel to the
bustling Rye Lane. Everything here seems to have
been chosen as much for its aesthetic as its (always
great) flavour: raw honey with minimalist labels;
old-school brands of alpine pasta; wicker baskets
of seasonal fruit and veg (though be warned, the
melons alone can go for over a tenner each). There
is even a section devoted to household (non-)
essentials like beeswax candles and Opinel picnic
knives. The clientele may not be as 'general' as the
name implies, but for well-heeled foodies this is a
paradise.

42

LULU'S

Deli by day, wine bar by night

The little sister to Herne Hill mainstay Llewellyn's restaurant, Lulu's is as cute – and a tiny bit naughty – as the name suggests. During the day, it's a stylish store and sandwich shop full of colourfully illustrated chocolate bars and swanky condiments, with an excellent edit of charcuterie and cheese. This is the kind of place where you pop in for a coffee and leave with pickles, kefir water and a ceramic jar of honey. Once 6pm hits, the sourdough crumbs are swept away, the lights go down and Lulu's transforms into a wine bar serving small plates and good vibes.

291 Railton Road, SE24 0JP
Nearest station: Herne Hill
lulus.london

LULU'S

10
10
8

Breakfast Martini
French 75
Suze & Tonic

3ea
9.5
8.5
7.5

9.5
14
15
17
18

Preserved Lemon & Chilli

...radish

43

LIFE OF FISH

More than just a (very good) fishmonger

What started as a lockdown fish stall has since become a series of successful south London stores. Fishmonger David is in charge of the catch of the day, laying out huge tiger prawns, whole rainbow trout and glistening sea bass. But that's only half the story. Whether you want to make paella or caviar blinis, they've got it. The shop has everything you could want to eat with fish, plus some stuff you can definitely eat without. Explore the array of independent products and discover some not yet spotted in any other London delis, like strawberries preserved in honey – just don't serve *those* with fish.

50 Abbeville Road, SW4 9NF
Nearest station: Clapham South
Other locations: Tooting, Earlsfield
lifeof.fish

44

DI LIETO

Low-key South London favourite

Di Lieto is the kind of place that locals want to keep all for themselves; on Saturday mornings there's already a queue out the door for their strong coffee and crisp cannoli. The deli section is small but has all the basics (if you can call fresh ricotta and rich unfiltered olive oil basic), with produce specials scrawled on paper bags and the short daily menu written on the blackboard. Time your visit to eat lunch in the cafe, where they'll bring over a bowl of fresh pasta coated in sweet pumpkin sauce and give you change from a tenner.

2 South Island Place, SW9 0DX
Nearest station: Oval
@di_lieto_bakery

45

GARCIA'S

Spanish supremo on Portobello Road

Half-deli, half-supermarket, Garcia's has been a family business for more than 70 years and has the old-school signage to prove it. The deli counter is packed with hams, chorizo, sheep's cheese, stuffed olives, membrillo and more. They have anything you could want for a Spanish feast, whether it's tinned Asturian bean stew or a massive bag of paella rice, but it's not just food – you can even pick up some of that Spanish shower gel you loved on holiday. And if your favourite tapas isn't here then try La Plaza, another quaint Spanish deli just up the road.

248–250 Portobello Road, W11 1LL
Nearest station: Ladbroke Grove
rgarciaandsons.com

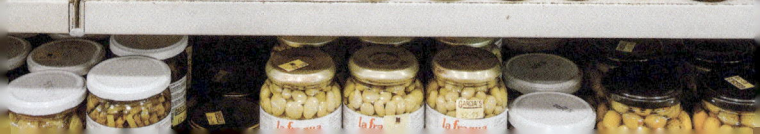

46

JAPAN CENTRE

Specialist food hall with hard-to-find eats

One of the few places in London that stocks those deceptively yummy matcha-flavoured green Kit-Kats, this basement supermarket and cafe has a brilliant selection of cupboard staples (with entire sections devoted to miso and dried seaweeds) and a number of small open kitchens serving up everything from fresh sushi to bao buns. There are freezers packed with gyoza and mochi ice cream too, but it's the fish counter – brimming with fatty tuna and grilled eel – that makes this a pilgrimage-worthy destination. Be warned, it's easy to buy lots (and it isn't cheap).

35b Panton Street, SW1Y 4EA
Nearest station: Leicester Square
Other locations: Westfield Stratford and White City
japancentre.com

47

SCANDIKITCHEN

All you need to fika like a Swede

Forget everything IKEA taught you about meatballs, this cheery cafe-deli is the place to go for a plate of real köttbullar with mash, lingonberries and gravy. Scandis flock here for tunnbrödsrulle (hotdogs wrapped in flatbread), smørrebrød (open sandwiches) and, of course, fluffy cinnamon buns to scoff down with a strong cup of filter coffee. At the back, pick up all the ingredients you need to recreate your own Nordic favourites, as well as other treats including Danish rémoulade mayo, little marzipan 'hoover' rum cakes and aquavit. They even sell reindeer meat, if you're feeling adventurous.

61 Great Titchfield Street, w1w 7pp
Nearest station: Oxford Circus
scandikitchen.co.uk

48

TOTALLY SWEDISH

Scandi comfort food

Swedes from across London and beyond flock here for a taste of home. From sourdough crisp-breads perfect for loading with mellow cheese to love-it-or-hate-it squeezable fish roe paste, this unassuming shop near Baker Street has everything (even super-salty lollipops, if that's your thing). There's Swedish Herbs (a home remedy also known as 'the long life elixir'), a mind-boggling array of crunchy pickles and liquorice, and even the correct sugar to sprinkle on your cinnamon buns, plus traditional wooden butter knives for the most chic way to make cloudberry jam on toast.

32 Crawford Street, W1H 1LS
Nearest station: Baker Street
Other location: Barnes
totallyswedish.com

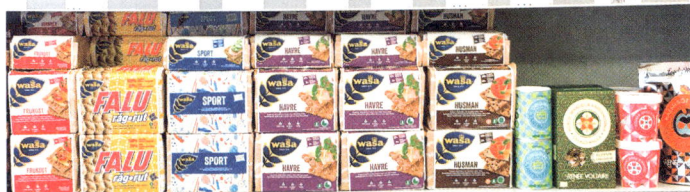

49

HONEY & SPICE

A beloved Middle Eastern offshoot

It's hard not to be inspired to cook something utterly delicious with the beautiful produce at this deli and cafe from the team behind the iconic restaurant Honey & Co. There's hard-to-come-by ingredients like rose water, smoked chilli oil, Persian limes, and their own fragrant spice mixes, plus what is possibly the best range of snacks in the capital (all made in-house) including preserved lemon and tahini cookies, seeded lavosh crackers and bars of sweet-and-spicy chocolate. Swing by for a plate of tagine or just a coffee, then grab one of the bright yellow tables spilling onto the street.

52 Warren Street, W1T 5NJ
Nearest station: Warren Street
honeyandco.co.uk/places/honey-spice

50

ATHENIAN GROCERY

Nostalgic Greek paradise

It's hard to argue with Athenian's claim that it's 'the oldest Greek deli in the UK' after paying them a visit – stepping inside feels like taking a trip back to 1952 when it first opened. This is a true celebration of Greek and Cypriot food with many indigenous ingredients you won't find elsewhere, like kolokasi (taro root) for making an authentically appetizing pork stew. There are breads stuffed with halloumi, sticky lemon and orange cakes, succulent unpackaged feta waiting to be ordered by weight, and many, many olives. If there's a cloche by the till with walnut and honey biscuits, buy as many as you can stuff into your pockets.

16a Moscow Road, W2 4BT
Nearest station: Queensway
atheniangrocery.co.uk

51

FRATELLI GRECI

A comprehensive Greek larder

In need of an escape to a Greek island? A trip to this small but friendly deli-cafe might not deliver total beachy bliss, but it's got enough Mediterranean flavours to satisfy at least some of those sunny daydreams. Whether you want to sit down and tuck into a moussaka or find premium ingredients to conjure up a sensational Greek dinner, this is the place. There are at least eight different kinds of feta, flaky filo pies, traditional hilopites (an underrated and rich-tasting Greek pasta), sprigs of healing mountain tea and an entire cellar full of wine – just perfect for recreating that holiday vibe.

26 Seymour Place, W1H 7NN
Nearest station: Marble Arch
shop.fratelligreci.com

52

GREEN VALLEY

Lebanese superstore

Fragrant Jordanian thyme, home-made orange flower jam, gooey cheesy knafeh cake made with noodles of pastry drenched in syrup – Green Valley is one of the tastiest spots in the little corner of the Levant that is the Edgware Road. Pass mini-mountains of baklava, barrels full of chillies, tubs of spices and dried fruit and stop by the brick oven turning out flatbreads stuffed with halloumi and kofta. Then hit up the counters of fresh salads, dips, mezze and hot food including moussaka, lamb shawarma baguettes and Egyptian koshari topped with fried onions and a spicy tomato sauce.

36-37 Upper Berkeley Street, W1H 5QF
Nearest station: Marble Arch
green-valley.co

53

BAYLEY & SAGE

Visual feast of seasonal produce

Abundance is the word that comes to mind with this chain of delightfully posh south-west London delis. There are ludicrously lofty stacks of fresh fruit, lemons almost as big as your head, monumental wheels of parmesan casually displayed on barrels and a cheese fridge you could get lost in. Then there's all their swanky ready meals – various kinds of creamy risotto, sea bream with lemon, spatchcock garlic butter chicken... and they even make their own truffle crisps to munch while you heat it all up. The selection is almost overwhelming, but don't sweat – remember, you can always come back for seconds.

33-34 Marylebone High Street, W1U 4QD
Nearest station: Bond Street
Other locations: Multiple, see website
bayley-sage.co.uk

WEY VALLEY
GREEN ASPARAGUS
£ 6,75 each
UK

First
of
The
Season

Vine Tomatoes
£3.50/kg

Strawberry
Cocktail
£15.50/kg

HERITAGE
TOMATOES
£ 8.50/kg
FRANCE

RAW
TOMATOES
£15.50/kg
SPAIN

Cherry on
Vine tomato
£ 20.00 kg
FRANCE

Jardin de Rabelais

Le Jardin de Rabelais

Le Jardin de Rabelais

LE JARDIN de R

54

PAUL ROTHE & SON

Old-school sandwiches and spreads

Is there such a thing as an English deli? The wonderful time warp that is Paul Rothe & Son might be the closest thing you'll find. Part-pantry, part-sandwich bar and cafe, this Marylebone institution has been buttering baps since 1900. Today, Paul (grandson of the founder) and his son still live here and run the show. They specialise in making sandwiches and selling jams, condiments (including five different types of Marmite) and preserves – stocking exhaustive ranges from their chosen brands, including Essex's Tiptree and Staffordshire's Cottage Delight. Look for the 'hot soup' sign outside and join the (thankfully fast-moving) lunchtime queue.

35 Marylebone Lane, W1U 2NN
Nearest station: Bond Street
@paulrotheandson

E & SON

Four Generations

35

Est. 1900

ENGLISH AND FOREIGN PROVISIONS

55

LUIGI'S DELICATESSEN

Italian fast food heaven

Whatever you do, don't visit this west London wonder on an empty stomach. Enter under the charming red awning, and you'll be confronted with tray after tempting tray of freshly prepped deliciousness: caprese, ravioli, meatballs, three types of lasagne, octopus salad, whole roasted poussin… the list goes on – and that's before we've started eyeing up the desserts. Even if you're not planning on throwing a big Italian party, a dollop of Luigi's homemade pesto will elevate any dish of pasta from mid-week mediocrity to a restorative repast.

349 Fulham Road, SW10 9TW
Nearest station: Gloucester Road
luigisdelicatessen.com

IMAGE CREDITS

Photography by *David Post* except for the images listed below:

Lina Stores (p.6), by Hugh Johnson; Lulu's (pp.8-9) ©Matt Russell; Lina Stores (second image) ©Lina Stores; The Quality Chop House and Shop, by Andrew Montgomery; I Camisa (first and third image) ©Marco Kessler; (second image), by Robert Evans/Alamy Stock Photo; Furanxo (all images), by Biel Moreno; Da Mario (all images) ©Marco Kessler; Natural Natural ©SAKESAKANA; Panzer's (first image), by Gile Christopher; (second and third images), by Jess Henderson; Melrose and Morgan (first image) ©Lesley Lau; (second image) ©Melrose and Morgan; De Beauvoir Deli (all images) ©Jon Day; Nourished Communities, by Yana Kasa; Salvino (all images) ©Marco Kessler; Provisions (all images) ©Laura Jalbert; Shalom Hot Bagels ©Shalom Hot Bagels; Oren, by Benjamin McMahon; Madeira Deli ©Ola O. Smit; Chatica ©Kennington Runoff; Persepolis (first image) ©Philippa Langley; (second image), by Yuki Sugiura; Borough Market, by Red Agency commissioned by Borough Market; Italo ©Sarah-Louise Deazley; Brindisa ©Brindisa; General Store (all images) ©Lesley Lau; Lulu's (all images) ©Matt Russell; Life Of Fish ©Rebel Ruth Design Studio; Di Lieto ©Claire Forster @londonhideout; Japan Centre (all images) ©Japan Centre; Totally Swedish, by juliavhill / Stockimo / Alamy Stock Photo; Honey & Spice (all images) ©Patricia Niven; Athenian Grocery ©Athenian Grocery; Paul Rothe & Son (all images) ©Rachael Smith.

CONTRIBUTORS

Sonya Barber is a freelance editor and travel, food and culture writer. She is a former editor at *Time Out London* and *Condé Nast Traveller* and the author of two books in the Opinionated Guides series by Hoxton Mini Press covering east London and day trips from the city.

Hoxton Mini Press is a small indie publisher based in east London. We make books about London (and beyond) with a dedication to lovely, sustainable production and brilliant photography. When we started the company, people told us 'print was dead'; we wanted to prove them wrong. Books are no longer about information but objects in their own right: things to collect and own and inspire. We are an environmentally conscious publisher, committed to offsetting our carbon footprint. This book, for instance, is 100 per cent carbon compensated, with offset purchased from Stand for Trees.

INDEX

An Opinionated Guide to London Delis
First edition

Published in 2023 by Hoxton Mini Press, London
Copyright © Hoxton Mini Press 2023. All rights reserved.

Text by Sonya Barber
All photography by David Post*
Copy-editing by Octavia Stocker
Proofreading by Gaynor Sermon
Design by Richard Mason
Production by Sarah-Louise Deazley
Production and editorial support by Georgia Williams

*Except for additional images credited on previous page.

With thanks to Matthew Young for initial series design.

Please note: we recommend checking the websites listed for each
entry before you visit for the latest information on price, opening times
and pre-booking requirements.

A CIP catalogue record for this book is available from the British Library.

ISBN: 978-1-914314-41-4

Printed and bound by OZGraf, Poland

Hoxton Mini Press is an environmentally conscious publisher, committed
to offsetting our carbon footprint. This book is 100 per cent carbon
compensated, with offset purchased from Stand For Trees.

For every book you buy from our website, we plant a tree:
www.hoxtonminipress.com

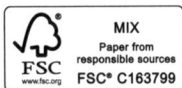

MIX
Paper from
responsible sources
FSC
www.fsc.org
FSC® C163799